Recareering: Dynamic Re-Direction

S. Thoman and Kef Hollenbach

CONTENTS

ACKNOWLEDGMENTS

Special thanks go to Karl F. Hollenbach for the use of his pamphlet "Recareering: Dynamic Retirement" as an outline for this book. His personal insight and work-life experiences have been a priceless asset to the authors for the duration of the project.

The publisher would also like to thank Cary Grant, Pedro J. Perez, and Michael S. Richter for permission to use their photos on the cover, www.morguefile.com/license/full

PROLOGUE

Karl F. Hollenbach's original pamphlet is an outline of the steps and discoveries he made when moving from one career-track to another over the course of fifty years. Since he is of the "Great Generation" which fought in World War II, he preceded the "Baby Boomers" who are now encountering similar situations.

As Hollenbach's publisher, we saw his outline pamphlet being beneficial to those Boomers facing voluntary, and involuntary, work life changes.

Since the original pamphlet was first published in 1993, many studies have been done on the recareering phenomenon, which validate and explain in-depth many of

Hollenbach's premises. While people today face similar challenges and opportunities, they may not be identical to those that Hollenbach encountered and resolved. Consequently, we explain various generalities with more in-depth, contemporary direction that can be applied to the world of today. Having known the author through several recareering events, we saw some of the mistakes from which he learned and how he applied those lessons to his next challenge.

Hollenbach's basic tenant is that every ending is a new beginning. Instead of leaving work behind for a no-work retirement, a person has the opportunity to apply their experiences and skills in a new direction; essentially going from something to a different something, a completely new activity.

A second tenant is subtle, in fact it is not even directly stated anywhere in the original pamphlet and may be difficult to discern in current studies, reports and discussions about recareering.

The second tenant of Hollenbach's original pamphlet, unspoken and almost metaphysical, is the alignment of a person's new direction with what they are most efficient and happiest doing - or what they are meant to do - their calling.

The International Standards Organization (www.iso.org) stresses many of the benefits of using international standards such as reducing costs by reducing waste, by minimizing errors, and increasing productivity. How ISO goes about this is by aligning activities. The more precise one activity aligns with another, the more efficient the entire process becomes.

Hollenbach outlined a few simple steps to finding effective, efficient, joyous recareering. Doing what you want to do, what you are meant to do, and at which you are good…very good at doing.

- Publisher.

"We periodically have to regroup, recalibrate, and reinvent ourselves."

~Jovita Jenkens~

RE-CAREERING DEFINED

The word "retirement" has become more and more difficult to define, especially for those baby-boomers who are making big voluntary changes later in life. At one time, retirement meant "an end to productivity" and is most often associated with taking things easy, stepping back and enjoying the fruits that your labor years have reaped. However, the word "retirement" is not exactly fitting for those people that leave one career path for another, whether or not financial gain is the motivation behind this change.

Twenty years ago, the word recareering mostly applied to those who were at retirement age, or those who entered major work life changes in mid to late life whether voluntarily or involuntarily. It implies a kind of mobility from one job to the next, but it can also be defined as moving on to the next phase of one's life to do the thing that they were *meant* to do.

It possesses a kind of ageless quality as more young people look to the future and imagine themselves thirty years from the present time. In this particular situation, these young people are already anticipating their re-careering move twenty, perhaps thirty, years before it happens.

Re-careering is a calling to your own true vocation, a return to the things that you are most passionate about and which you have not yet had the opportunity to truly pursue. Aligning one's skills, education, and work life experience with a new career regardless of age is perhaps the ultimate act of returning to happiness and satisfaction.

By learning and applying job skills earlier in life, one can prepare for the midpoint of life in which they learn new skills concerning that which they are passionate about, and finally, in later life, those skills may all come together in a new career that is spiritually and emotionally satisfying.

WHO RE-CAREERS?

Statistics show that younger people, particularly those in their early twenties, are far more likely to re-career than those folks who are at retirement age, specifically people who are age 65 or older. There are many different factors that play into this such as education, acquired job skills, and the financial stability that comes from pensions, 401(k)s, and other savings options. However, it is not unheard of (nor should it be) that people who are at retirement age, or in middle age re-career at a later junction in their life.

There are all sorts of reasons that a person might find himself or herself re-careering. Big life changes like moving from one place to another can create an opportunity for re-careering. A person who decides to return to school and get a degree later in life may decide to re-career to put their education to use.

There are also the less positive reasons such as business closure, lay-offs, and other types of involuntary career changes that are, unfortunately, not nearly as uncommon as they once were. However, even these kinds of major work life changes can be turned into opportunities with the right amount of ingenuity and positivity.

Then there are those folks who have discovered that they want something different, perhaps more fulfilling or less stressful than their current career and so they choose to take a different path.

By seeking out the things in life that are the most gratifying, enjoyable, and which make a person truly happy and then applying the skills of all their years spent at another career, a person may find that harmonious balance, that one thing that they were *meant* to do. With any luck, all of those years spent in the first, or even the second, career path have afforded them the chance to pursue it wholeheartedly, with all of their resources, skills, and determination no matter their age or what that calling might be.

This can seem to be easier said than done, especially with the economic worries of today. There is always the concern of how a person will provide for their families, and support himself or herself financially. It can be very daunting…this idea of pursuing that which makes you truly happy. That is why it is so important to consider what it is that you are *meant* to do, and that which you will be good at. If it is in fact, your true calling that you are chasing, how could you be anything but successful at it?

KNOWING YOURSELF

If this new career path is truly what you were meant to do, then it is perfectly reasonable to expect that many of the choices you've made and skills you've learned in your life already have aligned you with this big change. Perhaps you have been preparing yourself for it since beginning your work-life in early adulthood, and may or may not have realized it at the time.

A good working example of this would be to look back to the elective courses that you selected in college to earn credits toward a specific degree. Most likely, you selected courses that at least somewhat matched your interests and at which you felt you would do well. Perhaps you chose, intentionally or unintentionally, a career that reflected what you were good at, but you would really prefer to perform in a different way, such as starting your own business in the same field.

These are all examples of how one's work and education life combine to *prepare* you for the opportunity to re-career. This is where the term 'alignment" comes from. Whether consciously or unconsciously, we all make the work of preparing ourselves for that next "big something" in our life. After spending the earlier parts of our lives working to earn a wage, establishing financial stability, learning job skills and ethics, and reaching a mature emotional state, it makes perfect sense that we would move on to that which makes us most happy later in life.

Though it may be difficult to substantiate with research and statistics, this elusive aspect of recareering involves an individuals' personal progress that prepares them, grooms them if you will, for that one true calling, that "one something" that is gratifying spiritually, emotionally, and (hopefully) financially as well.

It is of immense joy, an unprecedented happiness that is yours to gain by recareering, and pursuing that which you were truly meant to do, the work for which everything else was preparation.

GUIDE TO RE-CAREERING

The most successful way of approaching the idea of re-careering is by asking yourself a series of relatively simple questions, truly reflecting on your answers, and listening quietly to what you have to say without interference from the logical or intellectual parts of your mind (at this point, it is the only thing that stands in your way).

What is it that I most love doing purely for the sake of doing it? This can seem like a very simple question at first, but again, if you let that logical and cautious part of your mind take over while answering it you will begin to question your abilities, and consequently, how successful you will be at pursuing this beloved activity as a career choice? It is important not to allow this to happen.

Consider what it is that you enjoy doing

more than anything, the thing that you will do regardless of whether there is financial gain involved. It can be something creative, something that you do in your spare time as a hobby such as cooking, sewing, writing, or making works of art, or something that you have stumbled across in your career path that is more conventional, but that gives you the utmost joy performing.

Focus on this action, whatever it may be, and ask yourself *"Is this something that I could do full time without sacrificing my enjoyment of it?"* This is an equally difficult question though seemingly simple, and perhaps just as important as the first question. You will have to discover whether the thing that you love so dearly will be something that you will continue to love if it should become your new career path. Sometimes the very enjoyment of a thing comes from that place where it is not an obligation or a requirement and this is very important to take into consideration before making your ultimate decision.

Finally, ask yourself, *"What are the steps to take to get there?"* This can be as simple as doing a little research into your chosen path, discovering what it is that you will need to do to begin, and reflecting on what you've already done that will lead you into this new career path. If you are thinking of becoming a writer for instance, how many old manuscripts do you have lying around that you could begin with? How many ideas for new works do you have that need only to be detailed, expanded, and written?

Perhaps these are things that you have already been thinking about, and you have intuitively discovered what it is that you want to do. If that is the case, then these questions will be less difficult for you to answer. That does not make the reflection period any less important. You will want the confidence of knowing within yourself that you are doing exactly what it is that you are meant to do, that which you have always known deep down, and begin taking the steps to arriving at that one true avocation.

The next step to recareering is to end all other activity that is not associated with your new career path. Whether this is the final act of retiring from your former career, or moving beyond the period of inactivity in between, this is the point where you embrace your new career, and begin working at it with all of your skills, education, and dedication.

Health is another consideration to take into account. You will want to make sure that you are doing everything possible to enable you to take this new path in your life. Get plenty of exercise, maintain a healthy diet, and devote plenty of time to other hobbies or enjoyments that will ensure your emotional satisfaction. These are all things that will help you be as fit as possible to continue in this new career, particularly if it less physical than what your old career was. Going from a very active career involving lots of moving around to sitting at a desk in your home office for instance is a big physical change and you will need to adjust your routine to ultimately ensure your happiness and success.

Remain positive! Do not allow yourself to dwell on the negative, and solely pursue that which makes you the most happy. If you avoid the things that depress you, then your physical, mental, and emotional health will benefit, and you will be better able to function in this new career path as well as your home life. Any recareering direction may involve difficulties and challenges; really opportunities to focus and learn. Remain positive!

Ask a child what they want to be when they grow up, they will give you all sorts of answers ranging wildly in scope, education and skill level..., and they do so without fear, self-doubt, or reservation because of what others will think. *That* is the kind of confidence that you want to attain in this new career.

RE-CAREERING AS AN ENTREPRENEUR

Perhaps by this point you've found yourself in something of a quandary…you already love your career, and cannot imagine yourself doing anything else. Perhaps you have already found that "one something" that you were meant to do and have been hard at it for most of your adult work life. Do it for yourself instead of someone else.

For some, the idea of going into business for themselves, especially later in life, can be frightening. It does not have to be, particularly if it is something that you have been functioning at for years in some other capacity. By now, you have learned the necessary skills, made the contacts, and probably know the ins and outs of the business itself. The rest … learning how to effectively direct, grow and enjoy your business is something that you will achieve just as much enjoyment from as the actual activity itself.

Jane Bryant Quinn, a financial expert and author of <u>Making the Most of Your Money NOW</u> (Bryant, 2013) puts the idea of "later in life" entrepreneurship like this. "A smaller percentage of retirees are able to turn their hobby into a business. However, the odds are against you if you pursue an entirely new line of work. You might find that it does not interest you enough, or that its demands are not a good fit. Not everyone is cut out to sell real estate on weekends or manage the local coffee shop."

This plays into the alignment between your skills, education, interests, and passions. Essentially, Quinn is stating that if it is not something that you are already familiar with, that you already enjoy, and that you have successfully functioned at in some capacity in the past, then going into business for yourself may not be the best choice for you at this junction in your life.

However, if it is something that you love, then all it would take is some research and perhaps a small start up investment to begin doing what you truly enjoy, and doing it for *yourself*.

You would not want to make a huge investment to begin with, and certainly not the bulk of your available resources, but it is possible to run a small, low-cost business out of your home part time, and still be free to enjoy leisure activities, and pursue other interests as well.

A great way to get started is to make a list of the aspects of the business that you are already comfortable with and about which are are educated. Then on the other side of the paper, make a list of the things that you are less familiar with that you would need to research.

Start from the beginning. Familiarize yourself with tax codes and potential tax breaks for small businesses. Open a separate business bank account, and keep good records of your expenses, and your income. It may even be possible for you to take a course at a local community college geared towards entrepreneurship.

If starting your own business doing what

you love would further the idea of a second career from a possibility to a reality, than you should do everything you can to make it possible. The entire premise is to find your true calling, pursue your dream, and if entrepreneurship is a part of your unique vocation, then you should explore it fully.

WHEN TO RE-CAREER

When is the best time to re-career? That depends solely on you, your skills, and your interests. If you have already retired from one career, and are spending your time in between inactively, then the time is absolutely now.

If you have not yet retired, and are waiting to decide what you will do next, then the best time will come to you, if you listen. The point at which you decide to explore the next chapter of your life will begin as a small whisper. Be sure to listen!

If you are in early to mid-adulthood and wish to prepare now for your retirement, timing is equally important, perhaps more so. You will want to balance your retirement savings with income so that you will have the option later on of pursuing your dreams with a new career choice.

Remember that recareering is not restricted to people already at retirement age. It can apply to anyone who wishes to, is motivated to, and is called to move from one career path to another. If you are not yet at retirement age, but have planned for your retirement, then it could be possible that you retire early from one occupation and move on to the next something in your life.

Retiring is like eating your seed-corn; recareering is planting it.

###

REFERENCES

Greengard, Samuel. *AARP Crash Course in Finding Work You Love.* USA: Sterling Publishing Co, Inc. 2008. Web. May 2013.

Jenkens, Jovita. *Get Out of Your Own Way: Create the Next Chapter of Your Life.* USA: Ajides Publishing. 2004

Johnson, Richard, Janette Kawachi, and Eric K. Lewis. *Older Workers on the Move: Recareering in Later Life.* Washington: AARP Public Policy Institute. 2009

Quinn, Jane Bryant. "Start Your Own Business" *AARP.org Bulletin.* Jan-Feb 2013. Print

Wikipedia contributors. "Adult learner." *Wikipedia, The Free Encyclopedia.* Wikipedia, The Free Encyclopedia, 4 May. 2013. Web. 27 May. 2013.

ABOUT THE AUTHORS

Kef Hollenbach was born and raised in Kentucky, USA. Going into business management after graduating from university yielded an eclectic set of experiences ranging from production work to mid-level management to business owner.

The very proud parent of a son and daughter and husband to a deeply appreciated wife, Kef revels in learning new things and visiting new places. With a strong propensity for sharing, he strives to weave his experiences and what he has learned into all of his writing.

S. Thoman grew up in eastern North Carolina, the oldest of three siblings. She has been writing creatively for over ten years, and works part time as an editor of various different types of fiction and non-fiction works.

She currently lives in Johnson City, TN with her partner and their two children.

www.ingramcontent.com/pod-product-compliance
Lightning Source LLC
Chambersburg PA
CBHW071558170526
45166CB00004B/1715